This Book Belongs To

Delectables
For All Seasons

Maryjo Koch

Spices

SWANS ISLAND BOOKS

CollinsPublishers
A Division of HarperCollinsPublishers

PUBLISHED IN 1997 BY
COLLINS PUBLISHERS
10 EAST 53RD STREET
NEW YORK, NY 10022-5299

LIBRARY OF CONGRESS CATALOGING-IN-PUBLICATION DATA
KOCH, MARYJO
    SPICES: DELECTABLES FOR ALL SEASONS / MARYJO KOCH
        P.   CM.
    ISBN 0-00-225068-3
    1. SPICES.   I. TITLE.
  TX406.K6323   1997
  641.3'383—dc20   96-43799

PRINTED IN CHINA
10 9 8 7 6 5 4 3 2 1

All plants are lamps
and their light
is their perfume.

VICTOR HUGO

pice

Variety's the very spice of life,
that gives all its flavour.

WILLIAM COWPER

Everything Nice

WHAT ARE SPICES? SIMPLY PUT, THEY ARE THE AROMATIC PARTS OF PLANTS — THE SEEDS, ROOTS, BUDS, BERRIES, BARK, AND FRUIT. AND MUCH MORE. SPICES ARE THE FLAVORS OF THE WORLD.

THE FAMILIAR COMFORT OF APPLE PIE, WITH ITS HOMEY RUSSET SCENT AND COZY CINNAMON FLAVOR, EVOKES CHILDLIKE PLEASURE. ITS BUTTERY CRUST, HOWEVER, CLOAKS CENTURIES OF DRAMA, HISTORY, AND GLOBAL UPHEAVAL SPARKED BY HUMANITY'S DESIRE FOR SPICES.

THE SPICES SO READILY AVAILABLE TODAY, SUCH AS CLOVES, NUTMEG, PEPPER, GINGER, AND VANILLA, WERE ONCE SO PRECIOUS THAT HOUSEHOLDS KEPT THEM IN DISTINCTIVE LOCKED BOXES. THE EXUBERANT USE OF SPICES IN COOKING ONCE INDICATED A HOST'S WEALTH.

HIGHLY VALUED IN TIMES PAST, SPICES OFTEN APPEARED IN DOWRIES AND WILLS.

IT IS SAID THAT THE QUEEN OF SHEBA BROUGHT KING SOLOMON NOT ONLY PRECIOUS STONES AND GOLD BUT ALSO EQUALLY COVETED SPICES. ASIDE FROM FLAVORING FOOD — AND, MORE IMPORTANTLY, PRESERVING IT — SPICES PLAYED IMPORTANT ROLES IN RELIGION, MEDICINE, AND POLITICS. THE SPICE TRADE BUILT SMALL NATIONS INTO EMPIRES, ALLOWING CITY-STATES LIKE VENICE TO BLOSSOM INTO WORLD-CLASS POWERS.

Nature's own spicy perfume so stirred our forebears' imagination that they sailed off to what they believed were literally the very ends of the earth in search of their pungent secrets.

A culinary journey to the land of spices takes us from our own kitchens, backyards, and gardens to faraway and exotic locales, where we join the families of the world in the eternal, daily ritual of mealtime.

According to the old proverb, laughter is brighter where food is best, for taste enriches all the senses.

# A Taste of Spicy Myths, Magic and Lore

Capitalizing on the mystical allure of spices, the Arabs closely guarded the secret of where they procured their merchandise. They maintained that spices like cinnamon came from paradise, and they warned the inquisitive of barbarous lands infested with poisonous snakes. Gullible medieval Europeans paid dearly for cargo such as nutmeg, which they used to make hypnotic potions and to treat bites from animals and mythic fire-breathing dragons. They also treasured aphrodisiac coriander and anise as essential ingredients in love potions.

Throughout Asia, turmeric is regarded as a magical plant because of its luminous golden color, which signifies enlightenment, illumination, and wisdom. Modern Buddhist monks use it to dye their ritual robes yellow, as saffron has become too expensive for such a purpose.

In preparation for marriage ceremonies, Indian Tamil women decoratively color their hands and feet with turmeric in much the same way Arab women do with henna.

It is thought that the ancient Persians used turmeric along with other yellow spices in their worship of the sun gods.

Medicinal spices:
comfort foods and kitchen cures

WHETHER FROM THE EAST OR WEST, FOLLOWING THE DICTATES OF MODERN MEDICINE OR ANCIENT WISDOM, MOST HEALERS ACKNOWLEDGE THE RELATIONSHIP BETWEEN A BALANCED DIET AND GENERAL GOOD HEALTH. EATING WELL CAN MEAN THAT THERE ARE NO BITTER PILLS TO SWALLOW. YOU PROBABLY HAVE AN UNDISCOVERED PHARMACOPOEIA OF SPICY REMEDIES IN YOUR OWN KITCHEN, AS GOOD FOR YOU AS THEY ARE DELICIOUS.

Licorice

NEXT TIME YOU CRAVE SOME STICKY, SWEET BLACK LICORICE, CHEW ON THIS: LICORICE HAS BEEN USED MEDICINALLY SINCE AT LEAST 500 B.C. AS AN ANTI-INFLAMMATORY FOR ARTHRITIC OR ALLERGIC CONDITIONS, AN EXPECTORANT FOR ASTHMA, A BLOOD CHOLESTEROL REDUCER, AND A RELIEVER OF GASTRIC UPSETS. IN CHINA, CHILDREN MUNCH ON THE ROOT TO IMPROVE MUSCLE GROWTH.

Pumpkin pie will taste even better when you know its classic nutmeg, clove, and cinnamon seasonings are genuine comfort foods. The essential oil of nutmeg can ease rheumatic pain and, like clove oil, dull a toothache. Clove oil is also an excellent antiseptic, and clove powder in food prevents vomiting.

Sprinkle a little cinnamon in your hot tea and toss in an orange wedge for a winter warm-up drink. Cinnamon eases all "cold" conditions, from stomach chills and arthritis to the common cold. Research has also shown that it helps balance blood sugar, a promising lead in the treatment of diabetes.

It happens to us all, that minor kitchen cut, so wash the wound and head for the spice cupboard. The essential oil of cinnamon, or a simple decoction of the spice, applied on a sterile cotton compress is a potent antibacterial and antifungal treatment.

Dried juniper berries add panache to stuffings, sauces, sausages, and pâtés. They also have ancient associations with ritual body cleansing and purification, and their essential oil was regarded as a cure-all for typhoid, cholera, and dysentery. The ancient Egyptians used it to remedy tapeworm, while modern herbalists recommend it for clearing up urinary tract infections.

Piggie Licorice

Licorice Chips

Soft Buttons

Black and White Mix

All Sorts

All Sorts

Snaps

Red Twist

Licorice Candies from "Cottage of Sweets" Carmel-by-the-Sea

La Pipette

Black Honeycomb

Licorice Toffee

Licorice Toffee

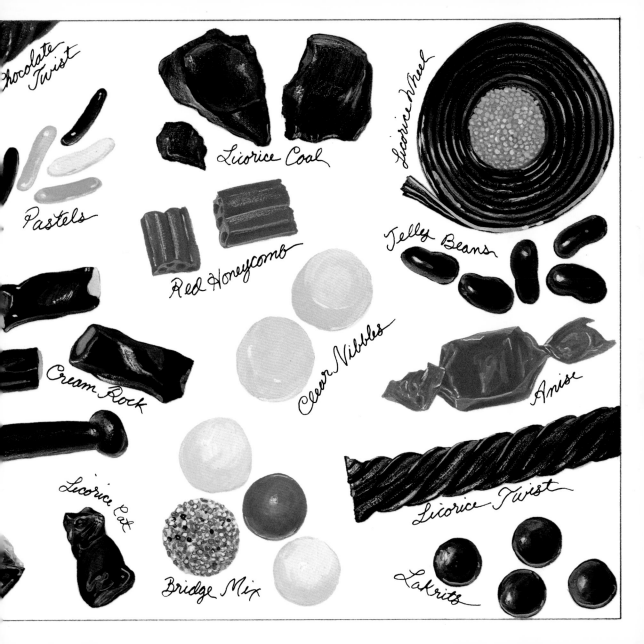

Chocolate Twist

Licorice Coal

Licorice Wheel

Pastels

Red Honeycomb

Jelly Beans

Cream Rock

Clear Nibbles

Anise

Licorice Cat

Bridge Mix

Licorice Twist

Lakritz

The History of Flavor

*M*OST LIKELY, NEOLITHIC HUMANS INVENTED THE ART OF SEASONING. AT SOME MOMENTOUS POINT LOST IN TIME, NUTRITION AND FOOD PRESERVATION ASCENDED THE THRONE OF GASTRONOMY. FIRST KNOWN AS AN IMPORTANT PRESERVATIVE, SALT WENT INTO THE COOKING POT (OR PIT) TO RESTORE LEACHED-OUT FLAVOR TO THE MEAT OR GRAIN IN BOILED STEWS OR PORRIDGES.

*M*ANY OF THE PLANTS ENCOUNTERED BY THE EARLY WANDERERS WERE PROBABLY BLAND, BUT SOME SURELY PLEASED THE PALATE. WHETHER THEY CHOPPED, DRIED, LEACHED, ROASTED, POUNDED, OR EVEN FERMENTED THEM, EARLY HUMANS WERE DESTINED TO DISCOVER WHICH PLANTS WERE SOPORIFIC, POISONOUS, USEFUL, CURATIVE, OR JUST PLAIN TASTY.

*R*OMANS ADORED THE VOLUPTUOUS FEEL OF FOOD:
*T*HE STING OF PEPPER, *T*HE PLEASURE-PAIN OF SWEET-AND-SOUR DISHES,
*T*HE SMOLDERING SEXINESS OF CURRIES.
— DIANE ACKERMAN

Indeed, wealthy Romans devoted their lives to all-night parties consisting of progressive meals. Staged as entertainments, each course was carefully designed to soothe or startle the taste buds. To heighten the effect, slaves blew exotic spices through pipes into the room, or some other delicacy infused with saffron would intentionally squirt out of the dish into the diner's face.

Medieval cuisine clearly reflected Roman tastes, but the Crusades expanded the European palate. Cinnamon, nutmeg, cardamom, mace, and cloves all made their way from the Middle and Far East into the castle kitchen.

While the European elite enjoyed a highly flavored and scented lifestyle, the general populace had to content itself with much less. The radical Puritans ultimately declared all spices too arousing and fled to the New World with their bland cuisine.

Soon, however, the seeds of gastronomic revolution were planted in the North American soil. Succeeding generations of explorers and immigrants carried new flavors with them and returned to their native countries with novel plants, spices, recipes, and techniques.

AVOR

Aspasia and Chloe,
and all of you who,
drawn by the Grecian artists,
make present beauties pale,
your lovely lips never savored
the suave delicacy
of meringue
concocted with vanilla
or rose water;
perhaps you never rose higher
than common gingerbread.

I weep for you!

JEAN ANTHELME BRILLAT-SAVRIN

Three Beans:

coffee

Vanilla

Chocolate

Traditional coffee lore links the bean with exhilaration and lucidity. Rapture and rebellion have been attributed to its tangy flavor and stimulating effects.

For the Aztecs, chocolate was the food of the gods. Montezuma's court drank 2,000 pitchers of it daily. The Itzás gave it to sacrificial humans to sanctify their journey to the next world. Chocolate also served as currency in pre-Columbian cultures: a hundred beans would buy a slave.

Long before the Spaniards came to Mexico, the Aztecs flavored their chocolate with the fruit of a climbing orchid named vanilla. They discovered the curing technique of sweating and drying the narrow, beanlike pods, thereby enhancing their musky flavor.

Separately and together, the flavors of this bean triumvirate form the foundation of the Western world's dessert vocabulary. One or all appear in virtually every after-dinner offering.

Accompanied by a vanilla-coffee-tinged chocolate fondue for dipping, an overflowing platter of fresh fruit and nuts is indeed a gift from the gods.

Make chocolate leaves by painting melted chocolate onto nonpoisonous leaves, cooling them in the fridge and peeling away the greenery. They are a delicate accompaniment to a cup of espresso sweetened with vanilla-laced sugar.

On the savory side, a square of semisweet chocolate placed in a stew at the last moment will eliminate any bitterness; the chocolate flavor will be almost unnoticeable. In the old Southwest, cowboys added coffee to their home-on-the-range BBQ grilled meats and beans.

In Spain and Italy, a traditional game sauce consists of tomatoes, garlic, onions, and chocolate. In Mexico, they add chili peppers, and it's molé, olé!

Rumor has it that vanilla-scented lobster is a favorite of mermaids.

Searching For The Spice Islands

When to them who sailed
beyond the Cape of Good Hope,
and now are past
Mozambic, off at sea north-east
Winds blow
Sabean odours from
spicie shoare
of Arabie the blest.
— JOHN MILTON

THE SEARCH FOR SPICE AT ANY PRICE HAD ALL THE ELEMENTS OF A SPECTACULAR SCREENPLAY: MYSTERY, INTRIGUE, BATTLES, ASSASSINATIONS, VILLAINS, HEROES, SAILING SHIPS, AND INTREPID TRADERS.

THE OPENING SCENE UNFOLDS AT THE COURT OF A CHINESE EMPEROR DURING THE HAN DYNASTY IN THE SECOND CENTURY B.C. A EUNUCH LEADS A VISITING HEAD OF STATE TO THE THRONE ROOM TO REPORT TO THE SON OF HEAVEN. BEFORE THE CURTAIN PARTS, THE SUPPLIANT IS OFFERED A PORCELAIN CUP, FROM WHICH HE TAKES AN AROMATIC, NAIL-SHAPED OBJECT AND PLACES IT IN HIS MOUTH. ONLY AFTER HE CHEWS THE HI-SHO-HIANG, "BIRDS TONGUE," SWEETENING HIS BREATH WITH CLOVES, WILL THE SILKEN CURTAINS BE DRAWN BACK SO THAT HE CAN MAKE HIS SPEECH.

THE CHINESE OBTAINED CLOVES — BY MANY ACCOUNTS ONE OF THE MOST POPULAR OF ALL SPICES — THROUGH TRADE WITH INDIA, WHICH HAD LONG USED THE SPICE TO FLAVOR FOOD. IN TURN, BRAVE INDIAN TRADERS HAD BROUGHT CLOVES TO THE SUBCONTINENT FROM THE MOLUCCAS, OR SPICE ISLANDS, IN INDONESIA. THERE THE EVERGREEN CLOVE TREE THRIVED NATURALLY IN THE WARM, HUMID CLIMATE.

FOR MANY CENTURIES, ARAB MERCHANTS CONTROLLED THE OVERLAND TRADE ROUTES TO INDIA. WHEN SAILORS CHARTED THE MEDITERRANEAN WATER ROUTES, ROMAN-CONTROLLED ALEXANDRIA IN EGYPT BECAME A COMMERCIAL CENTER. CLOVES, CINNAMON, PEPPER, CASSIA, AND OTHER SPICES SPREAD TO ALL SHORES OF THE SEA.

URGED ON BY TALES FROM PIONEERING TRAVELERS LIKE MARCO POLO, VENETIAN TRADERS CORNERED THE MIDDLE EASTERN SPICE MARKET BY THE THIRTEENTH CENTURY.

FED UP WITH THE EXORBITANT PRICES CHARGED BY THE VENETIAN SPICE MAFIA, THE SPANISH AND PORTUGUESE LOOKED SOUTHWARD IN HOPES OF FINDING AN OCEAN ROUTE AROUND AFRICA'S TREACHEROUS CAPE OF GOOD HOPE. MEANWHILE, CHRISTOPHER COLUMBUS LOOKED WESTWARD.

THE SEAFARING DUTCH WRESTED CONTROL OF THE SPICE ISLAND MONOPOLY FROM THE PORTUGUESE, AND THE SPICE SAGA CLIMAXED IN COLONIAL WARS AMONGST THE ENGLISH, DUTCH, SPANISH, PORTUGUESE, AND FRENCH ON FIVE CONTINENTS. THE CONFLICT FOREVER RESHAPED GLOBAL POLITICS AND PALATES.

Food for thought.

Tamarind

Green peppercorns

Elephant Garlic

Sugar Cane Cubes

Turmeric

Nutmeg

Chili Pepper

Pistachio

Licorice Root

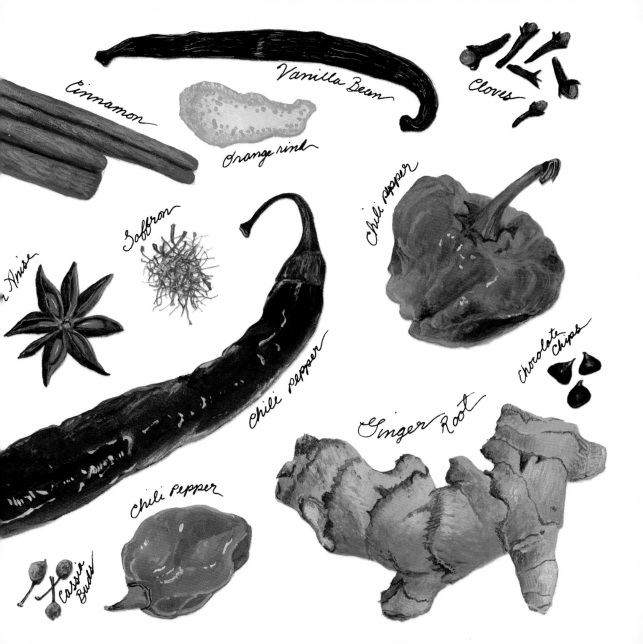

Cinnamon

Vanilla Bean

Cloves

Orange rind

Saffron

Chili pepper

Anise

Chili pepper

Chocolate Chips

Ginger Root

Chili Pepper

Cassia Buds

Chili Pepper

The Potted Pepper: Growing Your Own

MANY OF THE SPICES THAT ENCHANT OUR TASTE BUDS AND AWAKEN OUR SENSE OF SMELL ORIGINALLY HAIL FROM TROPICAL CLIMES. VANILLA, CHOCOLATE, CINNAMON, NUTMEG, CLOVES, TURMERIC, AND TAMARIND, TO NAME A FEW, ARE, FOR THOSE OF US FROM TEMPERATE ZONES, THE STUFF OF BOTANICAL DREAMS. EVEN TODAY, MOST OF THESE SPICES GROW SUCCESSFULLY ONLY UNDER ETERNALLY SULTRY SKIES OR IN RARIFIED GREENHOUSES, WHERE THEY MUST BE TENDED WITH EXQUISITE CARE.

OTHER SPICES, SUCH AS CARAWAY, CELERY SEED, CORIANDER, GARLIC, GINGER, JUNIPER, MUSTARD, ONIONS, SASSAFRAS, SAFFRON, STAR ANISE, AND NUMEROUS VARIETIES OF PEPPERS, THRIVE IN DIVERSE CLIMATES AND GARDEN SETTINGS.

LIKE CARAWAY, WHICH THE NORWEGIANS CALL "THE QUEEN OF POTHERBS," SOME OF THESE ARE SPIRITED BIENNIALS. OTHERS, LIKE MUSTARD, ARE HARDY INDISPENSABLE ANNUALS, THAT CAN BE PLANTED IN GARDENS, BEDS, BORDERS, AND POTS, AND ON TERRACES. A BIT OF EARTH, WATER, SUN, AND ENTHUSIASM CAN PRODUCE A PANTRY FULL OF SPICY PLEASURES.

MILD   SMOKY   SWEET   NUTTY   FRUITY

SPICY HEAT

SMOOTH HEAT

Many alliums—plants of the garlic and onion family, which includes roughly 300 species—are both ornamental and delicious. These plants are probably the most ancient spices cultivated by humankind.

Ranging from the pencil-thin, hotter-than-hot little devils called "ring of fire," to cayenne, paprika, the familiar sweet bell pepper, and beyond, all peppers are living sculptures. The vibrant, burnished colors of the fruits sing out from amid darkly gleaming green leaves. Living up to this vivid promise, peppers bestow sparks of personality on any food, from a humble glass of tomato juice to a lush slice of mango that accompanies a bit of grilled fish or chicken.

VERY SWEET

MEDIUM HOT

Preserving and storing spices basically requires nothing more complicated than a warm, dry, dark place with good ventilation, although roots and bark call for higher temperatures. Hang bundles of stems upside-down, encasing them in a perforated paper bag or muslin sack (no holes on the bottom!). The leaves will dry to a papery texture and the seeds and fruits will drop into the sack. Dried spices should be stored in airtight jars.

HOTTER THAN HOT

HOT

SEARINGLY HOT   HOTTEST   FIERY   BLAZING HOT

Decorative strings of gilded leaves and spices, dried chili peppers, fruits, nuts, bundles of cinnamon sticks, vanilla beans, and whole nutmegs can be assembled and then draped across the room as garlands or hung upon the Christmas tree.

making * Spicy Decorations

* Parent supervision recommended. Remember, most chilis are very hot.

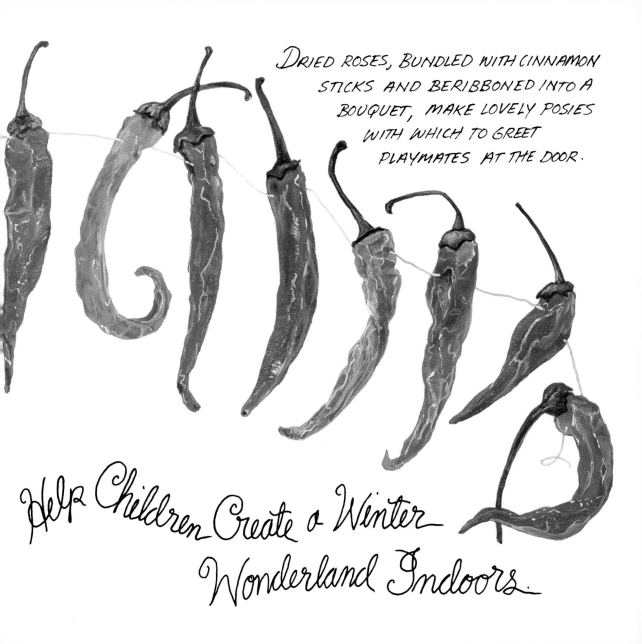

DRIED ROSES, BUNDLED WITH CINNAMON STICKS AND BERIBBONED INTO A BOUQUET, MAKE LOVELY POSIES WITH WHICH TO GREET PLAYMATES AT THE DOOR.

Help Children Create a Winter Wonderland Indoors.

Korean

Ancho

Bird's Eye

Chipotle

Red Chile

Bird

Anaheim

Serrano

Thai Red

Tepin Flor

Caribe

Thai Green

Santaka

Asian

Mulato

New Mexico

Habanero

Summer

Any artist knows that after a good bout of work one is both too tired and too excited to be of any use to anyone.

— STELLA BOWEN

Hot Stuff To Chill Out

The fruits of the perennial tropical shrubs known as the chili pepper are among the New World's great food gifts to humanity. Entire nations the world over have taken to this edible ambassador of heat and flavor.

Fill a tall glass with ice, pour in a blend of tomato and vegetable juice, add a bit of freshly grated ginger root, and top with a tiny chunk of a mild chili. Garnish with a celery stalk, and voila! A not-so-naive virgin Bloody Mary that will definitely pick you up. Chilies and sweet peppers are high in vitamins C and A. Though not quite as virtuous, this concoction is equally delicious spiked with gin or vodka.

Proof that hot peppers have antiseptic qualities, Africans employ them as a panacea for intestinal ailments. In fact, they roast their peppers to make them even stronger. African locals seem to suffer far less from digestive troubles than do wary travelers unaccustomed to diabolically hot dishes.

Add Gusto to your Gazpacho

1. PEQUIN   2. TEPIN   3. TUXTLA
4. CHILTEPE   ALL PEPPERS ACTUAL SIZE.

Summer soups of tomato, cucumbers, and bell peppers, spiced with garlic, onions, salt, pepper, fresh chopped green herbs, and a little olive oil can replenish energy spent enjoying the long, hot days to the fullest. Try adding a few mangos and jalapeño peppers for a little Miami spice, and serve it chilled in a frosted glass.

Mixed grill: make a meal of different kinds of grilled, roasted bell peppers—red, yellow, orange, green, purple.

Proceed with caution: carefully taste-test a few of the hot-headed pepper crowd before plunging in. Serrano, Anaheim, habanero, and chipotle, are among your options.

Dafne's Louisiana Voodoo: to chill someone out when temperatures and tempers rise, write the person's name on a piece of paper. Put the paper in the freezer, and you're guaranteed to cool off heated situations.

Autumn

To autumn
Season of mists and mellow fruitfulness,
Close bosom-friend of the maturing sun.

— JOHN KEATS

THE SPANISH CALL IT RED GOLD. THE WORLD'S MOST PRECIOUS SPICE, SAFFRON, IS IN REALITY THE TINY FEMALE ORGANS OF THE ARROGANT CROCUS FLOWER. OUNCE FOR OUNCE, THE SUNSET-SCARLET STIGMAS COST AS MUCH AS REAL GOLD.

BEAUTIFUL FRESCOES AT THE PALACE OF KNOSSOS, CRETE, SHOW A MAN GATHERING SAFFRON, STILL ABSORBED IN HIS TASK AFTER 4,000 YEARS.

Today, mid-October in the land of Don Quixote witnesses families spilling out into the vibrant purple crocus fields to harvest the blossoms. They must be picked within a few hours of the flowers' coming into full bloom, before they wilt and the saffron becomes worthless.

On the sweet side, float figs or a slice of chocolate torte on a golden pond of saffron-tinted crème anglaise.

Lauded as a flavoring, dye, digestive, hangover cure, and exhilarant, saffron is the stuff of legends. Zeus himself is said to have slept on a bed of saffron crocuses.

The gilded gourmet: in the Mediterranean tradition, saffron adds the mellow hue to Italian risotto, French bouillabaisse, and Spanish paella.

Winter

Winter kept us warm,
covering earth in forgetful snow...

— T.S. ELLOT

FORGETTABLE FRAGRANCES: IN MEDIEVAL TIMES, CLOTHES WERE WASHED ONCE ANNUALLY AT THE GREAT WASH. BETWEEN WASHES, WOOLEN ROBES AND VOLUMINOUS GOWNS WERE KEPT "FRESH" BY SWEET HERBS TUCKED UP INTO THEM AND CLOVE-STUDDED POMANDERS, OR SPICE BALLS, HUNG BETWEEN THEM IN CLOSETS.

THE ELIZABETHAN STILL ROOM — THE HOUSEKEEPER'S HERBAL AND SPICE WORKSHOP — WAS A PLACE OF GREAT ACTIVITY THROUGHOUT THE WINTER, WHEN SPICY MEDICINAL SIMPLES AND OTHER AROMATIC NECESSITIES AND NICETIES WERE PREPARED.

Orange Pomander

Press whole cloves into the skin of an orange. Set the cloves in a pattern around the orange with a space between each one to allow for shrinkage as the orange dries. Then roll the orange in a mixture of orris root and ground allspice or cinnamon. When covered with spices, tie a ribbon around it to suspend the pomander. Scent should last one year.

Spring

Spring has come again.
The earth is like a child
who knows poems.

— RAINER MARIA RILKE

Peeping out from the dark, rich earth soaked with spring rains are the first strawberries of the year.

To enhance the innocent flavor of strawberries, combine them with another berry: pepper, the regal king of spices. The glorious taste will reveal what epicures have known for centuries: a sprinkling of pepper makes flavors explode on the tongue.

A Provençal summer treat: a dessert of diced fresh peaches and pine nuts with a squeeze of lemon and a dash of sugar and pepper. Out of this world! For a South American twist add a few thin slices of fresh chili pepper to the peaches and serve as a fresh fruit salsa or as starter on a bed of dark green mesclun or fresh spinach.

The quest for pepper — as a spice and a preservative — dominated the spice trade for centuries. In fact, were it not for pepper, nations may not have built their colonial empires. Today, pepper still accounts for one-quarter of the global spice trade.

Such is the power of a plant.

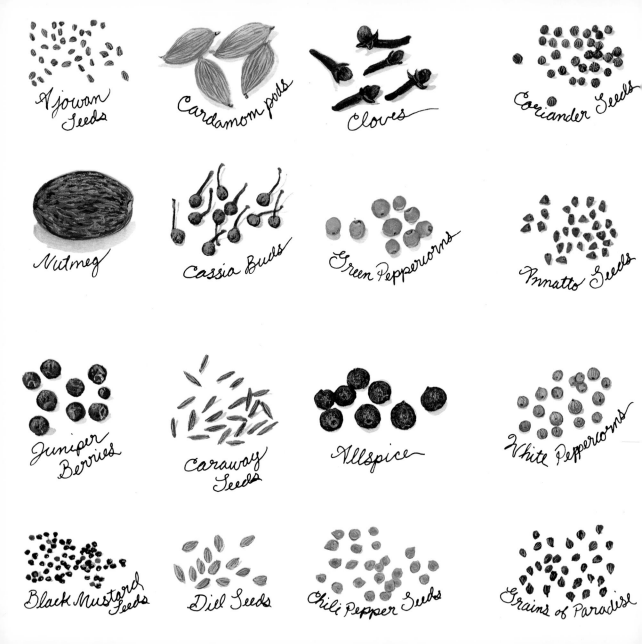

Ajowan Seeds

Cardamom pods

Cloves

Coriander Seeds

Nutmeg

Cassia Buds

Green Peppercorns

Annatto Seeds

Juniper Berries

Caraway Seeds

Allspice

White Peppercorns

Black Mustard Seeds

Dill Seeds

Chili Pepper Seeds

Grains of Paradise

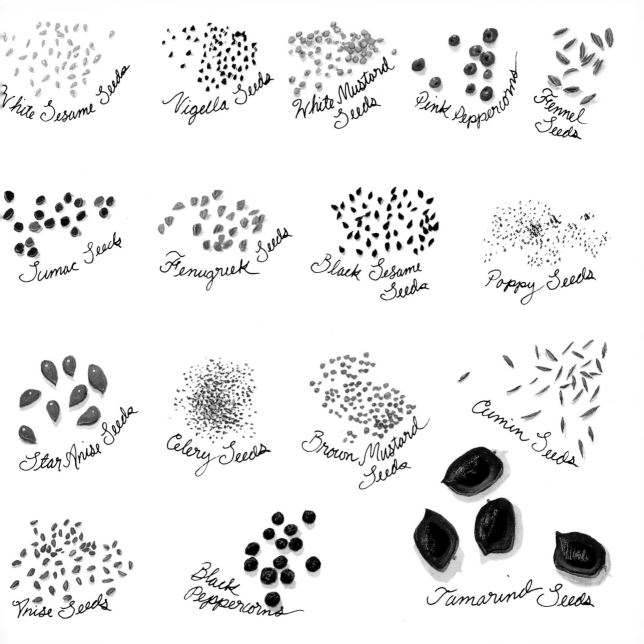

White Sesame Seeds

Nigella Seeds

White Mustard Seeds

Pink Peppercorns

Fennel Seeds

Sumac Seeds

Fenugreek Seeds

Black Sesame Seeds

Poppy Seeds

Star Anise Seeds

Celery Seeds

Brown Mustard Seeds

Cumin Seeds

Anise Seeds

Black Peppercorns

Tamarind Seeds

ALT

And then on every table
in the world,
salt,
we see your piquant
powder
sprinkling
vital light
upon
our food.
Dust of the sea, in you
the tongue receives a kiss
from ocean night:
taste imparts to every seasoned
dish your ocean essence;
the smallest,
miniature wave from the saltcellar
reveals to us
more than domestic whiteness;
in it, we taste infinitude.

PABLO NERUDA

Cornichon

Bread-and-Butter Chip

Tiny Kosher

Sweet Gherkin

Kosher Dill

Fresh Pickling Cucumber

Sweet Midget

More Than a Peck of Pickled Peppers

The pickling of food originated out of necessity rather than pleasure. But whatever the motivation for its creation, a pucker-up pickled cucumber is a wake-up call for the taste buds.

The preservative qualities of salt and vinegar also lend flavor and freshness to food. Almost any fruit or vegetable, and some meats and fish, can be pickled.

Where would an Italian antipasto be without pickled artichokes, eggplant, and peppers? Or French pâté without those adorable little cornichons? Or Korean food without kim chi, the pickled cabbage with firecracker-hot peppers?

Piccalilli, hailing from sultry India, is divine served with summer cold cuts. Diced mixed vegetables, such as cauliflower, carrots, string beans, pearl onions, red and green peppers, and celery, are pickled in salted vinegar with mustard, turmeric, ginger, and a touch of sugar.

Making your own pickles requires a little extra care, but is surprisingly less time-consuming than one might imagine.

The only problem with pickles: waiting. Most pickles' flavors mature in three to four weeks!

It quenches the thirst, revives, excites the brain and in old age awakes young love again.

REGIMEN SANITATIS SALERNO

Ginger: savory and sweet

According to Muslims, the joys of ginger are innumerable even in the afterlife in paradise. There, the virtuous are said to be honored by the houri, celestial courtesans who offer pleasure and ginger-flavored water to drink.

Back on earth, the magnificent rhizome has been used throughout Asia for more than 3,000 years. Dried, pickled, preserved in syrup, crystallized, freshly chopped, crushed, sliced, or pounded, ginger spread to the Middle East and Southern Europe well before Roman times. The Portuguese introduced it to Africa, and finally the Spanish carried it with them to the West Indies, where it continues to grow in fragrant abundance.

Make a simple tisane of grated ginger steeped in boiling water. Sip the infusion and nibble on a piece of crystallized ginger while you contemplate the plant's wondrous curative and culinary powers. Like cinnamon, ginger relieves all cold symptoms. It can also help with motion sickness and with morning sickness during pregnancy.

Ginger is the heart and soul of all gingerbread men and women.

In marinades, ginger has an affinity for soy sauce, citrus, garlic, and onions.

Chutneys, curries, pickles, vegetables, soups, and stews all come to life with the addition of freshly grated ginger root.

Ginger adds a clean flavor to seafoods and seems to lighten the fattiness of poultry (notably duck) and other types of meat.

Baked fruit, cakes, puddings, sweet breads, mulled wines, and spice teas are almost unimaginable without ginger.

Coriander

Anise

Nigella

Asafetida Compound

masala

Poppy Seeds

Dried Turmeric

Cumin

Cloves

The word curry evokes sun-drenched images of India and Southeast Asia, where steaming golden dishes offer fiery flavors complex and difficult to define. The term curry was supposedly coined by British colonials trying to describe the intricate masalas, or mixtures of spices that flavored sub-continental cooking. These same spices still are used to flavor food in the food-and-healing Ayurvedic tradition in India.

Chile Pepper

Ajowan

Cinnamon

Cardamom

Saffron

Sesame Seed

Pomegranate Seed

Ginger

Black Pepper

THE POWDERED AND PASTE BLENDS THAT DEFINE MASALAS ARE BOTH PERSONAL AND REGIONAL. IDENTIFYING VARIOUS MASALAS PAINTS A DETAILED TREASURE MAP OF THE SUBCONTINENT AND ASIA. MIXTURES MAY BE STRONG OR MILD AND MADE OF WHOLE OR GROUND SPICES THAT HAVE BEEN DRY-ROASTED IN A SKILLET TO ENHANCE THE FLAVORS.

Annatto

IMMIGRANTS FROM SRI LANKA HAVE ADAPTED THEIR CULINARY TRADITION TO THOSE OF THEIR NEW HOMELANDS IN THE WEST INDIES. THESE CREOLE MASALAS, CALLED "COLOMBOS," AFTER THE CAPITAL CITY OF SRI LANKA, MAKE VOLCANIC DISHES OF MIXED MEATS AND VEGETABLES STEWED IN COCONUT MILK – SOMETIMES WITH A LITTLE RUM ADDED.

Fenugreek

Galangal Root

Nutmeg

Mustard Seed

Garlic

'Tis garlic! It was a most tedious business,
not more than half a dozen shoots of garlic
being discoverable in the whole field;
yet such was the herb's pungency
that probably one bite of it by one cow
had been sufficient to season
the whole dairy's produce for the day.

— THOMAS HARDY

Garlic oil in a Guerlain perfume bottle

Garlic's potency leaves no one indifferent. Prized for at least 5,000 years for its culinary capability and medicinal prowess, it has been equally despised for its clinging, sulphurous aroma.

The Egyptian slaves who toiled to build the pyramids supposedly subsisted on garlic and onions. Likewise, Roman warriors ate a clove of garlic to keep up their strength during battle (imagine an entire legion panting with exertion). Yet in Rome, the Senate forbade anyone with tainted breath to worship in the temple of Sibil, and in Egypt, the priests condemned the masses of garlic eaters.

*L*OVERS ARGUE INCONCLUSIVELY ABOUT GARLIC, DIVIDING INTO TWO CAMPS: THOSE WHO MAINTAIN THAT THE AROMATIC VEGETABLE IS AN APHRODISIAC, AND THOSE WHO FLEE FROM FLAVORED KISSES. SCIENTIFIC ANALYSIS OF THE ORB'S CHEMISTRY SUPPORTS THE FORMER VIEW, BUT AESTHETICS IS A DIFFERENT MATTER ENTIRELY.

*G*ARLIC'S POWERFUL SULPHUR COMPOUNDS MAKE IT AN IMMUNE SYSTEM STIMULANT, AN ANTIBIOTIC, AND AN OLFACTORY OFFENDER. THE MORE PUNGENT THE PERFUME, THE MORE EFFECTIVE THE CLEANSING ACTION. STUDIES HAVE SHOWN THAT GARLIC LOWERS BLOOD PRESSURE, CHOLESTEROL AND BLOOD SUGAR LEVELS. ADOLESCENTS MAY BALK, BUT RAW GARLIC RUBBED ON THE FACE IS A WELL DOCUMENTED ACNE REMEDY!

*G*ARLIC'S GREAT CURATIVE POWERS HAVE EARNED IT A SUPERNATURAL REPUTATION. EVIL SPIRITS, VAMPIRES, WITCHES, AND WARLOCKS ARE ALL BOTH REPELLED AND REPULSED BY THE ALMIGHTY ALLIUM.

*T*HE FRENCH CHEF LOUIS DIAT WROTE THAT "GARLIC IS THE FIFTH ELEMENT OF LIVING, AND AS IMPORTANT AS EARTH, AIR, FIRE, AND WATER." INDEED, A CLOVE OF GARLIC AT THE BASE OF A ROSE BUSH WILL HELP IT THRIVE, FREE OF GREEN FLY AND OTHER PESTS, WITHOUT SPOILING THE FRAGRANCE OF THE FLOWERS.

A PROVENÇAL SAYING DUBS GARLIC "THE POOR MAN'S SPICE", BUT IT WAS THE RAVING, DECADENT ROMAN EMPEROR NERO WHO IS SAID TO HAVE INVENTED THE ULTIMATE GARLIC CONDIMENT, AIOLI.

*S*TART WITH EITHER HOMEMADE OR PREPARED MAYONNAISE AND MIX IN TWO TO FOUR CLOVES OF MASHED GARLIC, DEPENDING ON HOW STRONG YOU LIKE YOUR CONDIMENTS. SALT AND PEPPER TO TASTE, AND ENJOY. ADD CAYENNE PEPPER FOR A FIERY HIGHLIGHT OR CHOPPED PARSLEY AND CHIVES FOR A GREEN AIOLI. SEASON WITH BLENDED CURRY POWDER FOR A TASTE TRIP TO NORTH AFRICA.

Mustard Á La Mode

I desire your more acquaintance,
good master mustardseed.

WILLIAM SHAKESPEARE

Quick-growing, cold-resistant mustard is often one of the first seeds sown in the spring and the last plant to let go in the fall. In early spring, fluffy, flowering fruit-tree clouds floating above fields of yellow mustard promise warmth, sun, and good things to eat.

Black mustard seed has the strongest flavor, brown is easiest to harvest, and white mustard can be preserved for the greatest length of time.

Known since prehistoric times, mustard has manifold uses. In the first century A.D., Pliny listed forty remedies with mustard as the chief ingredient.

For example: one tablespoon of crushed mustard seed in warm water will induce vomiting in much the same way as do the dried roots and rhizomes of ipecac.

High performance: one tablespoon of dried mustard powder dissolved in hot water for a foot bath will warm and deodorize any athlete's feet, and oddly enough, a good hot foot soaking is said to relieve colds.

Going for baroque: Hot or strong, mustard has followed the general evolution of food fashions. It was spiced with cinnamon in the Middle Ages, spiked with chilies at the end of the Renaissance, scented with vanilla, orange, violet, or other floral fragrances during the late seventeenth century, and blended with champagne, capers, and anchovies in the oh-so-rococo eighteenth century. When a new flavor was discovered or came into fashion, it often showed up first in prepared mustard.

Make your own contribution to the history of food by inventing your own mustard recipe.

Start with about two ounces of dry mustard powder blended with one tablespoon of cornstarch or flour. Now the fun begins: add a total of four tablespoons of liquid, using any combination of water, cider vinegar, beer, brandy, milk, or something sweet like honey. Let the paste sit for 15 minutes to allow the flavor to develop. Then add the highlights.

Hot Cajun mustard: Blend in hot red pepper flakes, cumin, thyme, and paprika.

Cool green mustard: Toss in finely chopped fresh green herbs such as chervil, chives, parsley, tarragon, etc.

N Aureolin
0202 016 SL Series 4 A

Perfect color for painting mustard fields

Condiments *are culinary works of art*

Like the artists they are,
homemakers, chefs, and inventive folks with a
healthy appetite have created spicy sauces,
chutneys, relishes, jellies,
and flavored vinegars and oils
for every palate under the rainbow,
always carefully studying the harmony
and balance of their ingredients.
The scrutiny of time has made some
condiments immortal classics,
while others are passing trends.

Dijon mustard   Yellow mustard   whole grain mustard   sesame oil

mango chutney   green taco sauce   jalapeño sauce   pepper sauce

hot pepper oil   salsa   Ketchup   B.B.Q. sauce

soy sauce   Worcestershire   Szechuan sauce   hoisin sauce

Back To The Roots:

Horseradish and Wasabi

Horseradish root

Wasabi

WICKEDLY HOT GRATED HORSERADISH ROOT BITES BACK WITH ITS PEPPERY TASTE, CLEARING AND STIMULATING THE DINER'S PALATE IN PREPARATION FOR THE NEXT BITE. IT THUS MAKES AN IDEAL FLAVORING FOR HORS D'OEUVRES.

CAVALIER DINERS WHO UNDERESTIMATE THE PLANT'S PUNGENCY WILL EXPERIENCE TEARY EYES AND HOT FLASHES. THIS DEEP-HEATING ACTION, PARTICULARLY USEFUL FOR POULTICES APPLIED TO ACHY JOINTS, IS ONE OF THE PLANTS MANY MEDICINAL BENEFITS. HORSERADISH ALSO AIDS DIGESTION AND IS AN EXCELLENT SOURCE OF VITAMIN C, USED TO CURE OR PREVENT SCURVY. IT IS ALSO SAID TO IMPROVE LIVER FUNCTIONS.

HORSERADISH GROWS EASILY FROM ROOTS BOUGHT AT THE GROCER'S. PLANT THEM IN AN OUT-OF-THE-WAY CORNER IN THE GARDEN, BEARING IN MIND THAT EACH SEVERED ROOT WILL GROW INTO A NEW PLANT.

Green Gunpowder

Fresh wasabi root is sometimes called Japanese horseradish, although the plants are not botanically related. Fierce and stimulating, wasabi is indispensable in Japanese cuisine. Raw fish dishes like sashimi and sushi have very subtle flavors; wasabi's ability to clear the palate heightens appreciation for the ephemeral nuances.

While fresh wasabi is rarely seen outside Japan, the readily available dried powder can be reconstituted into a paste that is as explosive as the original.

Horseradish and Ketchup

Kids' Condiments

Kids' favorite: Horse around with make-it-yourself wild mustang ketchup slathered on BBQ hot dogs and mudburgers. The zippy dip also makes a great shrimp cocktail sauce.

Coarse-ground mustard and grated horseradish

Oompah-pah mustard: Add oomph to prepared, coarse-ground mustard in the form of a little grated horseradish. Grown-ups will find this condiment delectable with fish.

Thousand-spice-island Dressing

Thousand-spice-island dressing: Young castaways can add a tablespoon of mustang ketchup and a dollop of mayonnaise or aioli to basic vinaigrette. Chopped "seaweed" (parsley, dill, or chives) adds flavor to a crudité dip that makes raw vegetables irresistible.

NION

Take care to chop the onion fine. To keep from crying when you chop it (which is so annoying!), I suggest you place a little bit on your head. The trouble with crying over an onion is that once the chopping gets you started and the tears begin to well up, the next thing you know you just can't stop.

LAURA ESQUIVEL

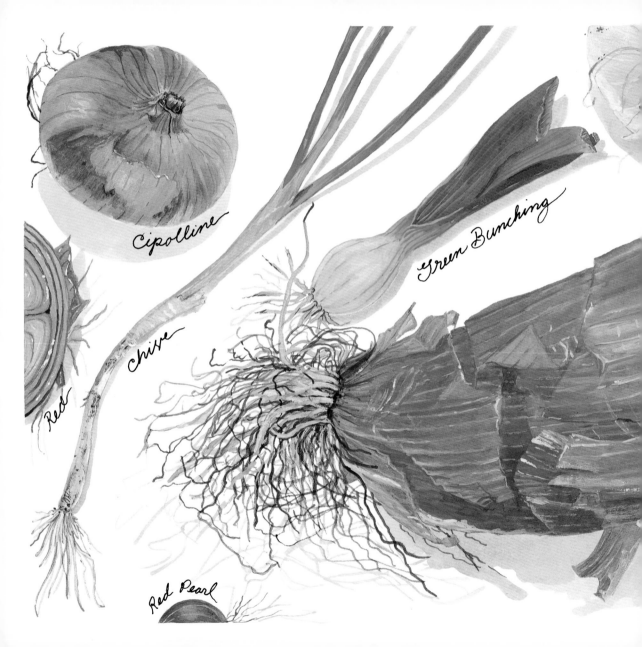

Cipolline

Green Bunching

Chive

Red

Red Pearl

White

Yellow

Pearl

Torpedo

Shallots

A Cook's Spice Chart

	Name	Used in	Form
	CHILI	FRESH TOMATO SAUCES, SAUSAGES, MEAT FISH, CORN, POULTRY, BEANS, AVOCADOS, ONIONS.	FRESH: RIPE, UNRIPE; DRIED. PROCESSED: CANNED, PICKLED.
	CINNAMON	COOKIES, CAKES, BREADS, STEWED FRUIT, PUDDINGS, STEWS, CURRIES, DRINKS.	DRIED: ROLLED STICKS, GROUND.
	CLOVES	HAM, PLUM PUDDING, MINCE MEAT, CAKES, GINGER BREAD, PICKLES, CHUTNEYS.	BUDS: DRIED WHOLE, GROUND.
	GARLIC	SAUCES, SOUPS, STEWS, ALL MEAT DISHES, SPREADS, FLAVORED BREAD, PICKLING, VEGETABLES.	DRIED: WHOLE, FLAKES, POWDER, SALT.
	GINGER	CHUTNEYS, PICKLES, CURRIES, SOY SAUCE, STEWS, VEGETABLES, SOUPS, CAKES, COOKIES, DRINKS, GINGERBREAD.	FRESH: WHOLE RHIZOME. DRIED: GROUND, SLICES, CRYSTALLIZED AND PICKLED.
	MUSTARD	SAUCES, SOUPS, STEWS, MAYONNAISE, COLD MEATS, POULTRY, ROASTS, STUFFED EGGS.	SEEDS: DRY WHOLE. GROUND: DRY. PREPARED AND FLAVORED.
	NUTMEG	CUSTARDS, SOUPS, PASTA, POULTRY, FISH, SAUCES, EGGNOG, VEGETABLES - ESPECIALLY SPINACH, CAKES, PIES, COOKIES.	WHOLE OR GROUND.
	ONIONS	SAUCES, SOUPS, STEWS, ALL MEAT DISHES, BREADS, PIZZA, SANDWICHES, VEGETABLES, PICKLING.	DRY: YELLOW, SWEET, RED, WHITE, PEARL, SHALLOTS; FRESH: SCALLIONS, CHIVES. GROUND: DRY FLAKED: DRY.
	PEPPER	SOUPS, CASSEROLES, STEWS, BUTTER, SAUCES, PÂTÉS, MEATS, SEASON SALAD, VEGETABLES, CRACKERS, CHEESE.	FRESH WHOLE BERRY. DRIED: WHOLE, CRUSHED, GROUND. PICKLED: WHOLE.
	SALT	ALL COOKING AND PRESERVING.	ROCK SALT: FINE, CRYSTAL. SEA SALT: FINE, CRYSTAL.

Ten Favorites

How To Store	Cooking Tips
WHOLE DRIED: TIGHTLY SEALED PLASTIC BAG GROUND: IN AIRTIGHT CONTAINER, IN COOL, DARK PLACE.	LONGER CHILI IS COOKED THE HOTTER THE FLAVOR. FOR MORE FLAVOR COMBINE DIFFERENT VARIETIES OF DRIED CHILIES AND GRIND TOGETHER FOR A FINE POWDER.
AIRTIGHT CONTAINER IN COOL, DARK PLACE, FOR BOTH STICK AND GROUND.	PINCH OF GROUND CINNAMON WILL ENHANCE MEAT STEWS; USE IN STUFFINGS MADE WITH DRIED FRUIT; USE STICKS IN MULLED APPLE SPICE DRINKS, COFFEE, TEA.
AIRTIGHT CONTAINER IN COOL, DARK PLACE.	STUD ONIONS TO FLAVOR STEWS AND SOUPS; STUD HAMS; ADD TO BOUQUET GARNI FOR LONG-COOKING MEAT DISHES.
WHOLE DRIED: COOL, DRY, WELL-VENTILATED AWAY FROM LIGHT. POWDER AND FLAKE: AIRTIGHT CONTAINER IN COOL, DARK PLACE.	RUB CRUSHED GARLIC AROUND INSIDE OF SALAD BOWL. CRUSHED IS MOST POTENT OF ALL. BAKE WHOLE HEADS IN OVEN, THEY'LL BECOME SWEET.
FRESH: REFRIGERATE-WRAP RHIZOMES IN PAPER TOWEL, ENCLOSE IN PLASTIC BAG. DRIED: STORE IN AIRTIGHT CONTAINER IN COOL, DARK PLACE.	GRATE AND ADD JUST BEFORE SERVING. USE DRIED GROUND IN COOKIES AND CAKES. USE PICKLED IN CHINESE CHICKEN SALAD.
PREPARED: IN REFRIGERATOR. SEEDS AND GROUND: IN AIRTIGHT CONTAINER IN COOL, DRY PLACE.	USE ON MEATS, HOT DOGS, IN SANDWICHES. USE PREPARED WITH SALMON. MAKE MAYONNAISE WITH PREPARED, NOT DRY. USE DRY FOR STEWS ADDED TO OIL IN WHICH ONIONS OR GARLIC IS COOKED.
IN JARS IN COOL, DARK PLACE.	ADD GROUND OR FRESHLY GRATED AT END OF COOKING.
COOL DARK VENTILATED PLACE. GROUND, FLAKED STORE IN AIRTIGHT CONTAINER IN COOL DRY PLACE.	USE RED FOR SANDWICHES AND SALADS. USE SCALLIONS IN SALADS, SOUPS OR STIR-FRIES. USE SHALLOTS FOR BEARNAISE SAUCE. PEARL ONIONS GO INTO STEWS.
DRIED: COOL, DARK PLACE IN AIRTIGHT CONTAINER AWAY FROM LIGHT. FRESH: AIRTIGHT CONTAINER IN REFRIGERATOR.	PEPPER AT END OF COOKING PROCESS FOR MAXIMUM FLAVOR. USE WHOLE PEPPERCORNS TIED IN CHEESE-CLOTH TO FLAVOR FOOD IN LONG-COOKING DISHES.
STORE IN DRY PLACE IN CLOSED CONTAINER. DO NOT USE METAL CONTAINER.	SALT WATER FOR BOILING VEGETABLES. ADD TO BREAD DOUGH TO BALANCE ACTION OF YEAST. SALT AFTER MICROWAVING. USE SPARINGLY. DO NOT SALT MEAT BEFORE COOKING. FISH CAN BE SALTED BEFORE COOKING.

# January

S	M	T	W	T	F	S

Protect your bay against cold winds.

Freshen the soil between evergreen plants.

Fresh horseradish roots are still available!

Keep plenty of seed in the bird feeders for feathered visitors.

Plant bare-root trees.

Drink hot spiced cinnamon tea to stave off colds.

February

S M T W T F S

Make valentines and send spice-scented notes to loved ones.

Bake heart-shaped vanilla shortbreads for loved ones nearby.

Check mailbox to see if seed catalogs have arrived.

If needed, transplant horseradish.

Plant garlic and tree onions.

March

S	M	T	W	T	F	S

Sow fennel seeds outdoors.

Transplant chives, Welsh onion, and other green herbs.

Celebrate the first day of spring.

April

S	M	T	W	T	F	S
		Sow seeds indoors: cumin.				
Sow seeds outdoors: anise, caraway, chervil, dill, fennel.						
		Plant bay if needed.				
		Take cuttings of fresh green herbs.				
If all possibility of frost has passed, plant potted pepper plants outdoors.						
Check your local nusery for a plastic plant-pot recycling program; if they don't have one, help them get started.						

May

S	M	T	W	T	F	S
		Sow outdoors : cumin.				
	Enjoy the harvest of fresh herbs and the first garlic.					
		Watch everything grow like crazy.				
Sprinkle cayenne pepper around the bases of plants to discourage slugs and snails.						
Build a tree house or climb a tree and admire the garden from above.						

June

S	M	T	W	T	F	S
			Begin drying extra herbs and spices.			
	make jams, jellies, marmalades, and chutneys as the fruits of the season ripen.					
	Celebrate the first day of summer: have a garden party. Serve spice tea.					

July

S	M	T	W	T	F	S

Pick a peck of peppers.

Make pickled everything!

Water the garden frequently.

Can luscious peaches, apricots, nectarines, and other fleshy fruits. Add cloves and cinnamon, and save for chilly winter days.

August

S	M	T	W	T	F	S

Read the "Just So Stories" by Rudyard Kipling aloud with little friends while lounging in the tree house or under the embrace of a shady tree.

Sip spiced, iced lemon tea.

Eat lots of chilies as a summer body coolant.

Paint and sketch the garden in full bloom.

Paint portraits of friends. (Renoir, when asked how he achieved such realistic flesh tones, said he just kept on adding color until he felt like pinching.)

Eat the first pickles!

September

S	M	T	W	T	F	S

Harvest and dry all herbs and spices.

Celebrate the first day of Autumn

Trim back perennial herbs.

Store all roots and seeds.

Watch for signs of animals preparing for winter.

October

S	M	T	W	T	F	S

Plan Halloween tricks and treats.

Paint blazing autumn foliage.

Dress plant beds with leaf mould.

 *ovember*

S	M	T	W	T	F	S

Prepare hot spots indoors for warm-blooded plants, such as potted peppers.

Continue to lift and store root crops.

Celebrate a spicy Thanksgiving with friends and family.

December

S	M	T	W	T	F	S

Celebrate the winter solstice. Light lots of spice-scented candles to make the house cozy.

While sending off Christmas cards to friends and family, write for new seed catalogs.

Decorate the house with spice-laden posies, garlands, and potpourri.

Sup on some of your spiced canned fruits and pickled vegetables, and dream of long, warm days in the garden.

Spice Notes

Thankyou

This book is akin to a fragrant spice cupboard — a rich mingling of diverse talents and contributions from healers, herbalists, gardeners, homemakers, perfumers, artists and always, good friends.

TO KRISTIN JOYCE OF SWANS ISLAND BOOKS, MY CHERISHED FRIEND AND SOLAR-POWERED PARTNER, WHO PLANTS THE SEEDS, DEALS WITH THE WEEDS AND TENDS THESE THRIVING BOOKS LIKE A PASSIONATE GARDENER.

To SHELLEI ADDISON AND HER EDITORIAL ARTS BUSINESS, FLYING FISH BOOKS. MY DEEPEST APPRECIATION FOR HER WRITING ABILITIES ESPECIALLY DURING A LONG AND CHALLENGING SOJOURN ABROAD. SPECIAL THANKS TO HER FAMILY— MICHAEL REX, ADDISON REX, DAVID DEAR, ISABELLE DEHAIS, AND THEIR LOVING FAMILIES FOR SUPPORT AND INSPIRATION DURING SHELLEI'S MANY MONTHS OF RESEARCH AND WRITING IN FRANCE.

To MY CHILDREN, WENDY AND JONATHAN AND ESPECIALLY TO SUNNY, FOR HER MAGNIFICENT GARDEN WHICH SUPPLIED SOME OF THE SPICES PAINTED IN THIS BOOK.

To MY MANY SUPPORTIVE FRIENDS AND FAMILY WHO KEEP ME LAUGHING AND ON MY TOES.

To MY DILIGENT AND TALENTED PAINTING STUDENTS WHO I HOPE WILL, ONE DAY, CREATE THEIR OWN BOOKS.

To OUR ORIGINAL PUBLISHER, JENNIFER BARRY WHO ACQUIRED THESE WORKS AND CONTINUALLY SUPPORTED OUR EFFORTS FOR COLLINS PUBLISHERS SAN FRANCISCO. WE ALSO THANK HER STAFF FROM MAURA CAREY DAMACION TO JENNIFER WARD AND JENNY COLLINS.

AND TO OUR NEW PUBLISHER, MARTA HALLETT AND HER EDITORIAL STAFF AT COLLINS PUBLISHERS JUST FRESHLY TRANSPLANTED IN NEW YORK. BEST OF LUCK!